The Storymaster's

PROFESSOR QUA...
WIZARD SC...
"WOULD YOU ...

FANTASY STORYTELLING
ADVENTURE GAME BOOK

By Oliver McNeil
Illustrations by Nick Vuimin
www.storymasterstales.com

Welcome, Adventurer!

You are about to take on a thrilling adventure quest of bold choices, puzzling conundrums, and silly questions!
Play with friends or on your own.
Good Luck!

Professor Quazimore

HOW TO PLAY

Pick someone to ask the questions and act as Professor Quazimore. They are also responsible for rewarding points but also deducting them if they think that your actions might have harmed you.

Take turns asking and answering the questions. Remember your answers, as they may change your later responses.

MAKE AN AMAZING STORY AS YOU GO!

The better the answer and story, the more points are rewarded.

HOW TO SCORE

The scorer will mark you from One-Ten.
One being Terrible, and Ten being AMAZING!
Extra points can be awarded for extra details using previously chosen items, creatures and skills.

If you are playing alone, you must determine how good your answer is, then congratulate yourself when you do well.

This book is split into TWO main segments.

PART ONE: DAWN OF THE HERO

1. CHOOSING CHARACTERS
2. FAMILIAR FRIENDS
3. MESMERISING MAGIC
4. EXCITING EQUIPMENT
5. CHARMING COMPANIONS

PART TWO: THE QUESTING

6. STARTING PLACES
7. DANGEROUS LOCATIONS
8. MAGICAL AREAS
9. HORRIBLE MONSTERS
10. CURIOUS CHARACTERS
11. HORRENDOUS HIDEOUTS
12. FRIGHTFUL FOES

At the end, add up the scores and look at your results. There are score sheets at the end of the book and to download for free from www.storymasterstales.com

NEW Bonus Questions at the back

SORCERER SCORES

ROUND | POINTS 1-10

1: CHOOSING CHARACTERS — 1:

2: FAMILIAR FRIENDS — 2:

3: MESMERISING MAGIC — 3:

4: EXCITING EQUIPMENT — 4:

5: CHARMING COMPANIONS — 5:

6. STARTING PLACES — 6.

7. DANGEROUS LOCATIONS — 7.

8. MAGICAL AREAS — 8.

9. HORRIBLE MONSTERS — 9.

10. CURIOUS CHARACTERS — 10.

11. HORRENDOUS HIDEOUTS — 11.

12. FRIGHTFUL FOES — 12.

TOTAL:

PART ONE:

DAWN OF THE HERO

1. CHOOSING CHARACTERS

"You must select which character you wish to become. Pick wisely, as you cannot change your mind later.

You can select only ONE!"

CHOOSE ONE. THEN TURN TO YOUR SELECTION

WITCH

WIZARD

BARD

RED-CAP (Animal Whisperer)

THE WITCH

WOULD YOU RATHER...

BE ABLE TO BREW A POTION TO MAKE YOU FLY
OR
CRAFT A POTION TO MAKE YOU INVISIBLE?

What would you do?

THE WIZARD

WOULD YOU RATHER...

MAKE YOURSELF THE SIZE OF A MOUSE
OR
MAKE YOURSELF THE SIZE OF AN ELEPHANT?

How would this be useful?

THE BARD

WOULD YOU RATHER...

BE ABLE TO SING A SONG THAT
MAKES PEOPLE CRY?

OR

SING A SONG THAT MAKES PEOPLE LAUGH?

What song would you sing?

THE RED-CAP (Beast Whisperer)

WOULD YOU RATHER...

BE ABLE TO TALK TO AN ANIMAL?

OR

BE ABLE TO TRANSFORM INTO ONE?

Which one and why?

What name will you give your character?

Where do they live?

How old are they?

2. FAMILIAR FRIENDS

"Now it's time to choose your familiar.

This creature is something you can use to help you on your quest.

You can select only ONE!"

CHOOSE ONE. THEN TURN TO YOUR SELECTION

PONY

CROW

CAT

BABY DRAGON

DOG

FAIRY

KITTEN

FERRET

PONY

WOULD YOU RATHER...

HAVE A PONY THAT CAN CARRY YOU AND YOUR BELONGINGS.

OR

A PONY THAT CAN FIT IN YOUR POCKET?

What will you call it?

CROW

WOULD YOU RATHER...

HAVE A CROW THAT TALKS TO YOU ALL THE TIME
OR
A SILENT CROW THAT GRABS THINGS FOR YOU?

What will you call it?

CAT

WOULD YOU RATHER...

HAVE A CAT THAT CAN TURN INTO A LION
OR
A CAT THAT CAN TALK?

What will you call it?

BABY DRAGON

WOULD YOU RATHER...

HAVE A DRAGON THAT CAN BREATHE FIRE
OR
A DRAGON THAT CAN FLY YOU OUT OF DANGER?

What will you call it?

DOG

WOULD YOU RATHER...

A DOG THAT WILL LIVE FOREVER
OR
A DOG THAT CAN TALK?

What will you call it?

FAIRY

WOULD YOU RATHER...

HAVE A FAIRY THAT WILL MAKE YOU FLY
OR
A FAIRY THAT CAN SEND PEOPLE TO SLEEP?

What does it call itself?

KITTEN

WOULD YOU RATHER...

HAVE A KITTEN THAT PLAYS ALL THE TIME
OR
A KITTEN THAT SLEEPS ON YOUR SHOULDER?

What will you call it?

FERRET

WOULD YOU RATHER...

HAVE A FERRET THAT DOESN'T SMELL OR BITE

OR

A FERRET THAT SMELLS SO BAD THAT ENEMIES RUN AWAY?

What will you call it?

Where is your new
pet friend going to live?

How will you feed them?

3. MESMERISING MAGIC

"Now it's time to choose a magical item for your quest. Turn over the page and select just ONE! Then go to the correct page to answer your question."

CHOOSE ONE. THEN TURN TO YOUR SELECTION

BOOTS OF LEAPING

BROKEN WAND

CLOAK OF INVISIBILITY

CRYSTAL WAND

MAGIC FLUTE

FLYING BROOMSTICK

MAGIC KEY

POTION OF WISDOM

BOOTS OF LEAPING

WOULD YOU RATHER...

BE ABLE TO DO ONE HUGE JUMP ONCE A DAY
OR
LOTS OF MEDIUM-SIZED JUMPS ALL DAY?

What could be your most impressive leap?

BROKEN WAND

WOULD YOU RATHER...

HAVE A WAND THAT WORKS WELL, BUT ONCE A MONTH TURNS YOU INTO A TOAD

OR

A WAND THAT ALWAYS CASTS RANDOM SPELLS, GOOD AND BAD?

What would be the best and worst spell that could happen?

CLOAK OF INVISIBILITY

WOULD YOU RATHER...

HAVE A CLOAK THAT COULD TURN YOU
HALF-INVISIBLE *Like a ghost.*

OR

A CLOAK THAT MAKES YOU INVISIBLE, APART
FROM YOUR FEET?

Where would you use it?

CRYSTAL WAND

WOULD YOU RATHER...

HAVE A WAND THAT CAN FREEZE A FOE INSIDE A CRYSTAL BLOCK
OR
A WAND THAT CAN GIVE YOU CRYSTAL ARMOUR?

Where would you use it?

MAGIC FLUTE

WOULD YOU RATHER...

HAVE A FLUTE THAT CAN MAKE ANIMALS SLEEP
OR
A FLUTE THAT FORCES PEOPLE TO DANCE?

What tune would you play?

FLYING BROOMSTICK

WOULD YOU RATHER...

HAVE A BROOM THAT CAN FLY
YOU TO THE MOON

OR

A BROOM THAT CAN TAKE YOU TO THE BOTTOM
OF THE SEA?

You can still breathe, but what would you do?

MAGIC KEY

WOULD YOU RATHER...

HAVE A KEY THAT COULD OPEN ANY BOX OR CHEST

OR

A KEY THAT COULD OPEN ANY DOOR?

What would be the best thing to unlock?

POTION OF WISDOM

WOULD YOU RATHER...

DRINK A POTION THAT WILL MAKE YOU READ FASTER

OR

A POTION THAT WOULD MAKE YOU REMEMBER EVERYTHING?

What would you love to learn?

Can you think of some cool magical items?

Try and create your own magical Would you Rather...

4. EXCITING EQUIPMENT

"Now you have your magical item; it's time for you to choose something to arm yourself in battle.

Pick One item, then turn to the correct page."

CHOOSE ONE. THEN TURN TO YOUR SELECTION

VORPAL SWORD

LION CLOAK

FLAMING BLADE

DRUID STAFF

DUELLING SWORD

BOW OF TRUE AIM

BEAR CLOAK

IRON SHIELD

VORPAL SWORD

WOULD YOU RATHER...

HAVE A SWORD THAT CAN CUT THROUGH ROCK
OR
A SWORD THAT CAN SING?

Swords should have a name. What will you call yours?

LION CLOAK

WOULD YOU RATHER...

HAVE A CLOAK THAT WOULD GIVE YOU THE STRENGTH OF A LION

OR

ALLOW YOU TO COMMAND LIONS?

What would be a cool way of using this power?

FLAMING BLADE

WOULD YOU RATHER...

HAVE A SWORD THAT IS ON FIRE
OR
A SWORD THAT CAN SHOOT FIREBALLS?

How would you stop setting fire to things by accident?

DRUID STAFF

WOULD YOU RATHER...

HAVE A STAFF THAT CONTROLS TREES
OR
ONE THAT CONTROLS RABBITS, BADGERS AND DEER?

Think of a cool situation where this would work well.

DUELLING SWORD

WOULD YOU RATHER...

HAVE A SWORD THAT IS FAST
OR
ONE THAT IS THE SHARPEST IN THE WORLD?

What would you need to be careful of?

BOW OF TRUE AIM

WOULD YOU RATHER...

HAVE A BOW THAT WOULD NEVER MISS ITS TARGET
OR
A BOW THAT SHOOTS LIGHTNING ARROWS?

Think of a cool situation where this would work well.

BEAR CLOAK

WOULD YOU RATHER...

HAVE A BEAR CLOAK THAT WOULD MAKE YOU AS STRONG AS A BEAR
OR
ONE THAT WOULD SUMMON A BEAR FRIEND?

What is the best thing about bears?

IRON SHIELD

WOULD YOU RATHER...

HAVE A SHIELD THAT WOULD PROTECT YOU FROM SWORDS

OR

A SHIELD THAT PROTECTED YOU FROM MAGIC?

What design would you paint on your shield?

Remember to try and use your previous choices to answer the new questions.

Try writing down what you have already.

5. CHARMING COMPANIONS

"You travel to the local town searching for someone to help you.

There are groups of people, but you must choose between just two. Make your choice, then answer your question."

CHOOSE ONE. THEN TURN TO YOUR SELECTION

PRINCE OR HIGHLANDER

MONK OR SCIENTIST

SOLDIER OR PIRATE

HUNTSMAN OR HIGHWAYMAN

PRINCE OR HIGHLANDER

WOULD YOU RATHER...

HAVE A RICH PRINCE WHO CAN BUY THINGS
OR
A FIERCE HIGHLANDER WHO FIGHTS BY YOUR SIDE?

Give whomever you choose a name!

MONK OR SCIENTIST

WOULD YOU RATHER...

HAVE A MONK WHO CAN STOP VAMPIRES AND ZOMBIES

OR

A SCIENTIST WHO CAN BLOW THINGS UP?

Give whomever you choose a name!

SOLDIER OR PIRATE

WOULD YOU RATHER...

HAVE A SOLDIER WHO CAN GUARD YOU
OR
A PIRATE WHO CAN FIND YOU TREASURE?

Give whomever you choose a name!

HUNTSMAN OR HIGHWAYMAN

WOULD YOU RATHER...

HAVE A HUNTSMAN WHO CAN TRACK MONSTERS AND ANIMALS

OR

A HIGHWAYMAN WHO CAN ROB FROM THE RICH AND GIVE TO THE POOR?

Give whomever you choose a name!

PART TWO!
THE QUESTING

6. STARTING PLACES

"Now, you must start your adventure.

You start in a friendly place.

Perhaps you can get some help."

CHOOSE ONE. THEN TURN TO YOUR SELECTION

THE WIZARD'S TOWER

STONE CIRCLE

THE CROWS NEST TAVERN

WOODEN FORT

WIZARD'S TOWER

WOULD YOU RATHER...

SLEEP IN A HAUNTED SCARY TOWER EVERY NIGHT FOR A YEAR BUT LEARN ONE HUNDRED SPELLS

OR

VISIT THE THE WIZARDS ONCE A MONTH AND LEARN A NEW SPELL EACH VISIT?

STONE CIRCLE

WOULD YOU RATHER...

STAND IN THE CIRCLE AND HAVE IT TAKE YOU TO A RANDOM PLACE IN THE KINGDOM

OR

DANCE IN THE CIRCLE AND SUMMON A THUNDERSTORM?

THE CROWS NEST INN

WOULD YOU RATHER...

ENTER THE TAVERN AND HAVE EVERYBODY
SCARED OF YOU

OR

GO INTO THE TAVERN AND HAVE EVERYONE
WANTING TO BE YOUR FRIEND?

WOODEN FORT

WOULD YOU RATHER...

BE TAUGHT HOW TO BE A BETTER FIGHTER BUT HAVE TO GET UP AT FOUR IN THE MORNING

OR

HAVE THE SOLDIERS MAKE JOKES ABOUT YOU FOR KNOWING MAGIC?

7. DANGEROUS LOCATIONS

"You have now reached a place of peril! Be careful which one you choose; it could be the last decision you make."

CHOOSE ONE. THEN TURN TO YOUR SELECTION

OLD CASTLE

MARCH OF SOULS

WALL OF THORNS

THE CAVE

OLD CASTLE

WOULD YOU RATHER...

GO INTO A CASTLE WHERE A MASTER VAMPIRES LIVE

OR

GO TO A CASTLE WHERE ONE HUNDRED WOLVES HAVE TAKEN OVER?

How would you fight them?

MARSH OF SOULS

WOULD YOU RATHER...

SPEND A NIGHT IN THE MARSH BEING HAUNTED BY GHOSTS

OR

HAVE TO SWIM IN THE STINKING SWAMP MUD FOR THREE HOURS?

WALL OF THORNS

WOULD YOU RATHER...

CLIMB THE WALL AND HAVE YOUR CLOTHES TORN TO RIBBONS

OR

CLIMB THROUGH THE THORNS AND CUT YOUR HANDS AND FACE?

THE CAVE

WOULD YOU RATHER...

ENTER A CAVE AND FIGHT A DRAGON
OR
GO INTO THE CAVE AND FIND A GANG OF GOBLINS

How would you fight them?

8. MAGICAL AREAS

"Well, I'm delighted you came through your first scary area in one piece. Now you are approaching a place of magic."

CHOOSE ONE. THEN TURN TO YOUR SELECTION

POTION ROOM

FLOWER GLADE

MUSHROOM FIELD

ALCHEMIST

POTION ROOM

WOULD YOU RATHER...

DRINK A POTION THAT MAKES YOU JUMP HIGH BUT GIVES YOU RABBIT EARS

OR

DRINK A POTION THAT MAKES YOU STRONG BUT TURNS YOUR SKIN BLUE?

FLOWER GLADE

WOULD YOU RATHER...

EAT A FLOWER THAT MAKES YOU SMELL LIKE CHOCOLATE

OR

EAT A FLOWER THAT MAKES YOU LIGHT AS A FEATHER?

MUSHROOM FIELD

WOULD YOU RATHER...

FIND A MUSHROOM THAT GLOWS, SO YOU CAN USE IT AS A LANTERN

OR

FIND A MUSHROOM YOU CAN EAT FOREVER AS IT GROWS BACK AFTER EACH BITE?

ALCHEMIST

WOULD YOU RATHER...

HAVE THE ALCHEMIST TURN SOMETHING YOU OWN INTO GOLD. What would that be?

OR

MAKE YOU A POTION THAT HEALS ALL WOUNDS AND CURSES?

9. HORRIBLE MONSTERS

"Oh no! You have discovered a horrible monster on your trip. Which one will it be, and how will you deal with it?"

CHOOSE ONE. THEN TURN TO YOUR SELECTION

GOBLINS

BLOOD-WOLF

GIANT SPIDER

TROLL

GOBLINS

WOULD YOU RATHER...

ATTACK THE GOBLINS BUT GET POISONED WITH A TERRIBLE ILLNESS

OR

HAVE THE GOBLINS FOLLOW, ANNOY AND LAUGH AT YOU FOR THE REST OF THE QUEST?

BLOOD-WOLF

WOULD YOU RATHER...

DEFEAT THE CREATURE AND BECOME A
BLOOD-WOLF EVERY FULL MOON.

OR

LEAVE THE CREATURE ALONE BUT KNOW THAT IT
WILL ATTACK THE NEAREST VILLAGE?

GIANT SPIDER

WOULD YOU RATHER...

GET TRAPPED IN THE SPIDERS WEB AND HAVE AN ARM EATEN BEFORE ESCAPING

OR

BURN THE WEB AND THE SPIDER WHO IS DOING YOU NO HARM?

TROLL

WOULD YOU RATHER...

BEFRIEND THE TROLL BUT HAVE HIM FOLLOW YOU EVERYWHERE. HE SMELLS AWFUL! *Very very Smelly!*

OR

ATTACK THE TROLL BUT LOSE YOUR COMPANION IN THE PROCESS?

10. CURIOUS CHARACTERS

"Now that you have escaped that peril, you have come across something that could be helpful."

CHOOSE ONE. THEN TURN TO YOUR SELECTION

DRUID

OWL LORD

FORTUNE TELLER

MASTER GIBBS

DRUID

WOULD YOU RATHER...

LEARN HOW TO TALK TO BIRDS
OR
LEARN HOW TO TALK TO TREES

What would they say?

OWL LORD

WOULD YOU RATHER...

BE ABLE TO HAVE AN OWL COME AND HELP YOU AT ANY TIME

OR

BE ABLE TO CHANGE INTO AN OWL?

FORTUNE TELLER

WOULD YOU RATHER...

SEE INTO THE FUTURE. *What would you see?*
OR
LOOK INTO THE PAST?
What time would you look back to?

MASTER GIBBS

WOULD YOU RATHER...

HAVE THE ARMS, STRENGTH, AND HAIR OF A CHIMPANZEE

OR

BE ABLE TO CLIMB LIKE A CHIMPANZEE BUT ALSO HAVE ITS FACE?

11. HORRENDOUS HIDEOUTS

"You have found the lair of a terrible enemy, but which one?"

CHOOSE ONE. THEN TURN TO YOUR SELECTION

PIRATE TOWN

DUNGEON

RUINED KEEP

GRAVEYARD

PIRATE TOWN

WOULD YOU RATHER...

TRAVEL TO A PIRATE TOWN DRESSED AS A PIRATE AND TRY TO BLEND IN

OR

FIGHT A GANG OF PIRATES BUT RISK BEING CAPTURED?

DUNGEON

WOULD YOU RATHER...

ENTER A DUNGEON FULL OF TROLLS AND GOBLINS.

OR

ENTER A DUNGEON FULL OF ZOMBIES AND LIVING SKELETONS?

RUINED KEEP

WOULD YOU RATHER...

ENTER THE KEEP AND FIND A CAPTURED PRINCESS
OR
ENTER THE KEEP AND FIND A CAPTURED PRINCE?

GRAVEYARD

WOULD YOU RATHER...

FIND THAT THE GRAVEYARD HAS CURSED TREASURE

OR

DISCOVER THAT YOU HAVE BEEN TURNED INTO A GHOST?

11. FRIGHTFUL FOES

"You have come across one of the villains of this Kingdom. How will you use your powers, knowledge and friends to defeat them? The best answer gets double points! Choose your enemy!"

CHOOSE ONE. THEN TURN TO YOUR SELECTION

SHADOW KING

SCARLET SORCERER

EVIL ENCHANTRESS

BABA YAGA

SHADOW KING

WOULD YOU RATHER...

HOW WOULD YOU STOP THE SHADOW KING?

USE YOUR WEAPONS AND STRENGTH
TO DEFEAT IT.
OR
USE YOUR MAGIC AND CUNNING TO DEFEAT IT?

SCARLET SORCERER

WOULD YOU RATHER...

HOW WOULD YOU STOP THE SCARLET SORCERER?

USE YOUR WEAPONS AND STRENGTH
TO DEFEAT HIM.
OR
USE YOUR MAGIC AND CUNNING TO DEFEAT HIM?

EVIL ENCHANTRESS

WOULD YOU RATHER...

HOW WOULD YOU STOP THE EVIL ENCHANTRESS?

**USE YOUR WEAPONS AND STRENGTH
TO DEFEAT HER.**

OR

USE YOUR MAGIC AND CUNNING TO DEFEAT HER?

BABA YAGA

WOULD YOU RATHER...

HOW WOULD YOU STOP THIS EVIL WITCH?

USE YOUR WEAPONS AND STRENGTH
TO DEFEAT HER.

OR

USE YOUR MAGIC AND CUNNING TO DEFEAT HER?

CONGRATULATIONS!

You have finished your quest.
Add up your points to see how well
you have done!

SORCERERS SCORES

Points	Hero Level
0-20	APPRENTICE
21-50	ROGUE
51-100	VILLAGE HERO
101-120	KING'S CHAMPION
121-200	LEGEND
201-300	HERO GOD

BUT THERE IS MORE!

WOULD YOU RATHER

BONUS ROUND!

JUST FOR FUN

Not for points... unless you want to!

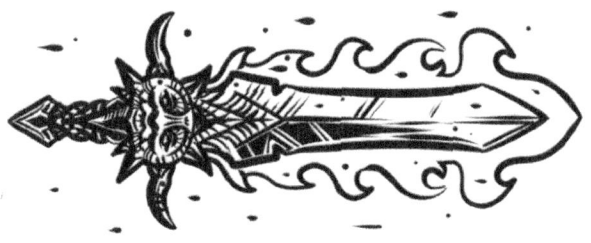

1. WOULD YOU RATHER...

HAVE A GOBLIN AS A BROTHER
OR
A TROLL FOR A FATHER?

2. WOULD YOU RATHER...

HAVE HAIR THAT REACHES YOUR FEET
OR
HAVE NO HAIR AT ALL?

3. WOULD YOU RATHER...

HAVE GOAT HORNS GROWING FROM YOUR HEAD
OR
HAVE THE LEGS OF A GOAT?

4. WOULD YOU RATHER...

ONLY BE ABLE TO EAT FISH
OR
ONLY BE ABLE TO EAT CHEESE?

5. WOULD YOU RATHER...

BE AS STRONG AS A GIANT BUT BE TINY AS A PIXIE
OR
BE AS MAGICAL AS A PIXIE BUT AS BIG AS A GIANT?

6. WOULD YOU RATHER...

BE ABLE TO MAKE THINGS FLOAT IN THE AIR
OR
MAKE OBJECTS COME ALIVE?

7. WOULD YOU RATHER...

CUT DOWN TREES WITH YOUR HANDS
OR
MAKE TREES GROW WITH YOUR MIND?

8. WOULD YOU RATHER...

HAVE GRASS INSTEAD OF HAIR
OR
SKIN MADE OF ROCK?

9. WOULD YOU RATHER...

HAVE SUPERHUMAN HEARING
OR
SUPERHUMAN SIGHT?

10. WOULD YOU RATHER...

A WAND MADE OF BONE THAT CAN BRING BACK
THE DEAD
OR
A WAND OF LIGHT THAT CAN ACT LIKE A TORCH?

11. WOULD YOU RATHER...

OWN A CROWN THAT CAN MAKE YOU A KING OR QUEEN
OR
A SPELL TO MAKE EVERYONE EQUAL?

12. WOULD YOU RATHER...

BE ABLE TO RUN AS FAST AS A PANTHER
OR
TO BE ABLE TO FLY LIKE AN OWL?

13. WOULD YOU RATHER...

BE ABLE TO TURN INTO A WOLF
OR
BE ABLE TO TALK TO BEARS?

14. WOULD YOU RATHER...

HAVE TO CLEAN UP AFTER A PIG FOR A WEEK
OR
SLEEP ON AN ICE BLOCK FOR ONE NIGHT?

15. WOULD YOU RATHER...

HAVE A WIZARDS HAT GLUED TO YOUR HEAD
OR
WALK IN THE SNOW WITHOUT YOUR CLOTHES?

16. WOULD YOU RATHER...

CHANGE YOUR NAME TO RUMPELSTILTSKIN
OR
CHANGE IT TO BUMBLE-FLUFF?

17. WOULD YOU RATHER...

RESCUE A BEAUTIFUL PRINCESS FROM AN EVIL DRAGON
OR
RESCUE A BEAUTIFUL DRAGON FROM AN EVIL PRINCESS?

18. WOULD YOU RATHER...

PUT STICKY MUD ON YOUR FACE FOR A DAY
OR
SIT IN A BATH OF ICE FOR TEN MINUTES?

19. WOULD YOU RATHER...

LIVE TO BE ONE HUNDRED YEARS OLD
OR
LIVE TO BE ONE THOUSAND YEARS OLD?

20. WOULD YOU RATHER...

HAVE HANDS WITH WORMS FOR FINGERS
OR
HAVE SNAKES INSTEAD OF HAIR?

21. WOULD YOU RATHER...

LIVE IN A LAND OF DOGS
OR
IN A LAND OF CATS?

22. WOULD YOU RATHER...

MEET SANTA CLAUS
OR
OR THE TOOTH FAIRY?

23. WOULD YOU RATHER...

OWN A CHAIR THAT CAN WALK
OR
A CARPET THAT FLIES?

24. WOULD YOU RATHER...

BE ABLE TO SMELL FEAR
OR
BE ABLE TO SMELL THE TRUTH?

25. WOULD YOU RATHER...

HAVE A GHOST HAUNT YOU
OR
A ZOMBIE LIVE WITH YOU?

26. WOULD YOU RATHER...

DRINK FROM A WITCHES CAULDRON
OR
HAVE A SWIM WITH A SNAKE?

SORCERER SCORES

ROUND	POINTS 1-10
1: CHOOSING CHARACTERS	1:
2: FAMILIAR FRIENDS	2:
3: MESMERISING MAGIC	3:
4: EXCITING EQUIPMENT	4:
5: CHARMING COMPANIONS	5:
6. STARTING PLACES	6.
7. DANGEROUS LOCATIONS	7.
8. MAGICAL AREAS	8.
9. HORRIBLE MONSTERS	9.
10. CURIOUS CHARACTERS	10.
11. HORRENDOUS HIDEOUTS	11.
12. FRIGHTFUL FOES	12.

TOTAL:

SORCERER SCORES

ROUND	POINTS 1-10
1: CHOOSING CHARACTERS	1:
2: FAMILIAR FRIENDS	2:
3: MESMERISING MAGIC	3:
4: EXCITING EQUIPMENT	4:
5: CHARMING COMPANIONS	5:
6. STARTING PLACES	6.
7. DANGEROUS LOCATIONS	7.
8. MAGICAL AREAS	8.
9. HORRIBLE MONSTERS	9.
10. CURIOUS CHARACTERS	10.
11. HORRENDOUS HIDEOUTS	11.
12. FRIGHTFUL FOES	12.

TOTAL:

SORCERER SCORES

ROUND | POINTS 1-10

1: CHOOSING CHARACTERS — 1:

2: FAMILIAR FRIENDS — 2:

3: MESMERISING MAGIC — 3:

4: EXCITING EQUIPMENT — 4:

5: CHARMING COMPANIONS — 5:

6. STARTING PLACES — 6.

7. DANGEROUS LOCATIONS — 7.

8. MAGICAL AREAS — 8.

9. HORRIBLE MONSTERS — 9.

10. CURIOUS CHARACTERS — 10.

11. HORRENDOUS HIDEOUTS — 11.

12. FRIGHTFUL FOES — 12.

TOTAL:

DOWNLOAD MORE SORCERER SCORES FROM

WWW.STORYMASTERSTALES.COM

Other Storymaster Tales Games

Weirding Woods
Dracodeep Dungeon
Threatlore Town
Tome of Terror
Fantasy & Folklore ABC

All available from AMAZON

Printed in Great Britain
by Amazon